M. Longden

Edited by Debbie Lines

ISBN 0 86112 597 5
Published by Brimax Books Ltd, Newmarket, England 1990.
Printed in Hong Kong

SURVIVAL
IN THE
ICE AND SNOW

by Jane and David Glover
Illustrated by Brian Watson

Brimax Books · Newmarket · England

Acknowledgements
Daily Telegraph Colour Library: 10/11
Eric Hosking: 35UL (D Hosking)
Frank Lane Picture Agency; 11 (C Carvalho); 19U (R Wilmshurst);
24 (S McCutcheon); 29U (T Whittaker); 32 BL (D Hosking); 32C (C Carvalho)
NHPA: 32 UFL (B Hawkes); 32 UL (H Palo Jr); 32 UR (P Johnson);
34U (D C Blossom); 37 (R J Van Aarde)
Oxford Scientific: 25 (D C Fritts); 33 (D Allan); 34B (D Allan); 35B (D Allan)
Planet Earth Pictures: 12 (B Merdsoy); 19B (R Matthews); 28U (D J
McChesney); 28B (F J Camenzind)
Survival Anglia: 14/15 (J Bennett); 29B (D & M Plage); 32UR (M Tracey);
32BR (M Tracey)
Zefa: 35R (R Hummel)

All kinds of animals live and raise their families in the coldest parts of the world.

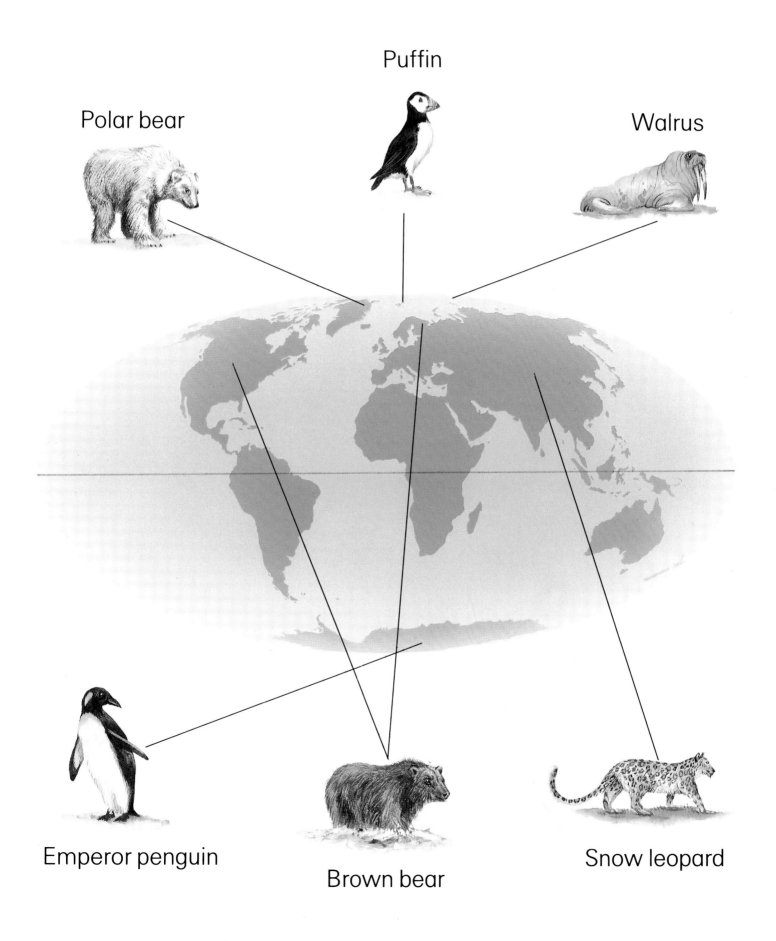

Puffin

Polar bear

Walrus

Emperor penguin

Brown bear

Snow leopard

The Arctic

It is so cold in the Arctic, the top few metres of the sea are frozen and this forms pack ice. The North Pole is in the middle of this frozen ocean, on the pack ice and not on land.

The pack ice is home for polar bears and harp seals. Arctic foxes follow polar bears very closely to eat their leftovers.

polar bear

harp seal

Whales swim under the ice and come up for air where there is no ice on the water.

Walruses and grey seals lie on the shore and dive into the water to feed, or for safety, when polar bears come near.

walrus

arctic fox

Polar bears

Polar bears are the hunter of the Arctic. Their creamy white fur is good camouflage against the snow. They are kept warm by a thick layer of blubber and their fur is well-oiled to keep out water when they are swimming. The soles of their feet are hairy, giving them a good grip on the slippery ice.

Polar bears wander over the pack ice searching for food. They mainly hunt seals, but will also eat dead whales and walruses. Their sense of smell is so good, they can find the breathing holes that seals make, even when the holes are covered by snow. The polar bear waits by the hole until a seal comes up for air.

An adult female polar bear has cubs every two or three years. She digs a special den in the snow where she has her babies in the middle of winter. She normally has two. They are smaller than kittens to begin with. The mother polar bear does not let her cubs leave the den until spring arrives and the cubs are much bigger.

Seals

Harp seals like to live in large groups. They spend the summer feeding on the small fish and crabs that live in the sea around and under the pack ice. They rarely come near the land. At the end of the short Arctic summer they travel south to their breeding grounds. The pups are born on the ice. They are covered in thick fur to keep warm. After about three weeks the pups begin to lose their thick fur and are left to look after themselves.

Ringed seals are the commonest seals in the Arctic. They spend the whole year feeding under the ice around the Arctic shores. Seals are mammals, not fish, so every few minutes they must come up for air. They make breathing holes in the ice and use their strong teeth to keep them open.

In early spring, the female seal scrapes away the snow around a breathing hole to make a small cave. Her pup is born here. At first it cannot swim and she must take care that it does not fall into the water.

The summer sun melts the top of the snow cave. The mother and her pup lie beside the breathing hole. The pup learns to swim and fish by diving in and out of the water while the mother looks out for polar bears.

Walruses

Walruses like to live in large groups. Great herds feed in the shallow waters around the Arctic shores. They use their tusks and whiskers to scrape up clams and worms from the sea bed. They suck the clams from their shells.

After a large meal the walruses use their tusks to pull themselves onto the shore to lie in the sun.

In a walrus family there is one bull, two or three cows and several calves. The families live in herds and in winter the walrus herds travel south to find a place where the sea is not completely frozen.

The calves are born in May just before it is time to travel north again for the summer. The calves ride on their mothers' backs or cling to their breasts for the journey north.

As the calves cannot feed themselves until their tusks are grown, they feed on their mothers' milk for the first eighteen months of their lives.

Whales

Three kinds of whale live and breed in the Arctic Ocean. They are the bowhead, the white whale and the narwhal.

The bowhead whale is a huge whale, reaching about 18m (58ft) in length, but it feeds on the smallest animals, called crustaceans. Instead of teeth, its mouth is filled with hundreds of plates of whalebone, called balleen, which work like a sieve. The whale swims along with its mouth open catching millions of tiny crustaceans. It then pushes the water out with its tongue, leaving the food behind.

Bowheads were once common, but now they are rare as man has hunted them nearly to extinction. They were killed for the balleen, to use in corsets, umbrellas, even furniture and also for their blubber.

narwhal

bowhead w

The white whale and narwhal are toothed whales and feed on fish and squid. They are much smaller than the bowhead, only reaching a maximum of 5m (16ft). Even though they have a very similar diet, they do not compete for food as the white whales prefer shallow water, while the narwhals are found almost always in deep water.

Male narwhals are the only whales with tusks. The spiral 'tusk' is a tooth that grows up to 2.7m (8ft) long.

White whales are born dark brown or blue grey. But the colour fades and they turn white at maturity.

white whale

Arctic Birds

Summer in the Arctic is very short, but many birds migrate to the surrounding tundra to nest and breed.

The ivory gull stays in the Arctic all year round. It is the only gull with all-white feathers. It is a scavenger, feeding on scraps left by polar bears and Arctic foxes.

Brent and Canada geese nest and rear their young on the tundra, along with Bewick swans. They fly south when winter comes and their young have grown.

The snowy owl has a mostly white plumage. It lives and nests on the tundra but moves south if the weather is very bad. It hunts by day, for lemmings and hares.

The ptarmigan is another all-white bird of the tundra, but it is only white in winter. The rest of the year it is a mottled colour to match its background.

The Arctic tern is a beautifully streamlined gull with narrow, pointed wings and a long tail. It feeds on small fish and other sea creatures. It catches them by hovering above the water and then diving quickly into the sea to seize the food in its beak.

Hundreds of terns nest together on beaches at breeding time. They are protective of their young and if a great skua or other bird tries to steal a chick to eat it, the terns in the colony will attack the bird. The young birds grow very quickly, as summer here is short. When the summer ends they must begin their long journeys south. Some go all the way around the world to the Antarctic – the longest journey made by any creature.

Many more birds live in the cold north near the Arctic. These are the seabirds. They live most of their lives at sea, only returning to land briefly to breed and rear their young.

The skuas are the pirates of the air. These dark-feathered birds chase other sea birds to make them drop their prey, which they then catch, and eat themselves. It also preys on other birds' nesting colonies, eating any unattended young or eggs. It nests in colonies at the foot of cliffs. Usually 2 eggs are laid, and both parent birds care for the young.

Kittiwakes nest in enormous colonies of thousands of birds, usually at the top of high cliffs. The male and female build a nest using seaweed and plants and cement it to the cliff ledge with mud. Both birds look after the young when they are born.

Puffins are very well known seabirds. They are black and white birds, with red legs and feet and a brightly coloured bill. They nest in abandoned rabbit holes or dig their own short tunnels on the grassy tops of cliffs. They usually have one young and it is fed until the parents consider it is well advanced. Then the parents fly far out to sea to feed. The young will follow when it is hungry enough.

Puffins feed on fish and shellfish and can carry several fish at a time back to the nest. It is a good flier but when on land it waddles because it has very short legs.

Tundra

The cold lands around the Arctic ocean are called tundra. No trees grow here because the ground is permanently frozen. During the brief summer, the top few inches of the soil thaws allowing short plants to grow, but the ground is always waterlogged because the frozen ground underneath does not allow any water to drain through. Insects hatch to live brief lives and breed before the next winter.

Herds of musk oxen and caribou in North America and reindeer in Europe migrate here for the summer to breed.

Lemmings and hares have to keep a careful lookout for the snowy owl who will take young hares or lemmings to feed its own young.

polar bear

wolves

lemming

wolf

Wolves follow the migrating herds of caribou and reindeer. Wolves live in family groups in packs. They hunt stray deer and smaller animals such as mice and fish.

Some of the smaller animals live all year round on the tundra. Lemmings make tunnels and burrow under the snow, and during spring will start to produce young in these snow burrows.

Arctic hares and foxes live all year round on the tundra. The fox also goes onto the pack ice, following the polar bears, scavenging from their leftovers. Both the hares and foxes, like the polar bear have fur on the soles of their feet to grip when walking on ice and to keep their feet warm.

reindeer

musk ox

arctic fox

arctic hare

The musk ox, the biggest animal to live on the tundra, is well adapted to life in harsh conditions. It has a very dense undercoat which is fully waterproof and insulates against the cold. The topcoat is long and thick and protects the ox from snow and rain.

Musk oxen live in large groups and are very protective of the young when they are born. If danger threatens, such as wolves or even polar bears leaving the pack ice, the musk oxen form a circle facing outward. With their horns lowered, this is a very effective defence.

Reindeer, or caribou as they are called in North America, are the only deer where both male and female have antlers. The females' antlers are a little smaller than the males.

The male gathers groups, or harems, of females in autumn. The following spring the doe has a single young, occasionally two. The young fawn is able to run with the herd within a few hours of being born.

The small lemmings, up to 15cm (6 inches) long, are active day and night. They eat grass, shrubs and mosses, and clear passages and runways under the winter snow in their search for food. As they start to breed early in the year, a female may have as many as eight litters of six babies each time, all through the summer. Some years this can cause a population 'explosion' and the young go off in their hundreds looking for new feeding grounds. This is when many are caught by the hunters, or they drown in rivers and lakes.

Mountains

Many animals have adapted to living in the mountainous parts of the world. Mountains are cold places to live, especially in winter when the cold weather is more severe. Mountains usually have snow on them. This reflects the sun instead of absorbing it, making it even colder. There is not much oxygen in the air at great heights, which is why climbers carry oxygen with them. It is also extremely windy, making it even colder.

No plants can grow at the very tops of mountains so there are no animals there. Further down, as plants are able to withstand the cold and can send down roots into cracks and grow, small animals live and breed.

brown bear

ibex

yak

Large animals such as the ibex, yak or mountain sheep and goats graze all year in the mountains, but move down to the lower slopes when winter arrives.

These attract the carnivores such as the snow leopard in Asia or the lynx in North America. Both of these big cats will follow the plant eaters as they move down the slopes for the winter.

The brown bear, in Alaska in North America, spends winter asleep in a cave. This is not a true hibernation, as it can wake up if the temperature outside rises or drops too far.

mountain goat

snow leopard

lynx

mountain sheep

The favourite food of the brown bear of Alaska is salmon. It catches the fish from the river. When autumn comes, the bear changes to a diet of fruit and berries to prepare for the long winter ahead. The female bear breeds every two to three years and she has one to four very tiny young. They stay with their mother for a year or more. Some species of brown bears are rare now because they have been hunted by man.

The snow leopard in Asia lives in meadows above the treeline. The treeline is the point where trees can no longer grow, because it is too cold and there is very little soil for the roots. The snow leopard stays in the meadow all summer preying on the mountain goats and sheep that graze in the meadows, following them to lower slopes in winter.

Snow leopards usually live alone, but a female leopard will be seen with her cubs. Usually, she has two or three who start to go with her on hunting trips when they are about two months old.

Yaks are large animals, the male can stand 2m (6ft) at the shoulder. The female is somewhat smaller. Both males and females have heavy horns which they use to defend themselves and their young. They form a circle facing outward with the young in the middle.

Small herds are made up of one male, several females and their young. Bachelor bulls wander in small groups of two or three animals.

The yak has been domesticated for centuries in Tibet, where it is used as a pack animal and to pull carts. It also provides milk and meat and its hair is woven into cloth.

Antarctic

Antarctica is the coldest land on earth. It is covered by ice and snow all year round and has been for 25 million years. The south pole is in the middle of Antarctica. One part of the land is covered by ice over 2.5km (1½ miles) thick.

Millions of penguins and seals live around the coast and on the nearby islands, but inland it is too cold for animals to survive. Also there are no predators on land such as polar bears or foxes. This is because there have been no land links with the neighbouring continents for animals to cross.

skua

whale

penguins

leopard seal

The main food for many Antarctic creatures is the krill in the seas. Krill are tiny shrimp-like creatures. There may be so many in a shoal that they make the sea look red.

Many seabirds fly south to the Antarctic to feed during the summer and to breed but they tend to stay on the islands around the mainland.

Whales come to the Antarctic seas to feed in the summer. They return to warmer waters further north to breed. They live on the reserves of fat they have built up and may not eat again until they return to Antarctic waters the following summer.

snow petrel

wandering albatross

adélie penguin

emperor penguin

Birds

The birds that live and breed in Antarctica are well adapted to life here.

The most famous are the penguins. Seven species of penguins live here. They are the gentoo, chinstrap, adélie, macaroni, rockhopper, king and emperor penguins. Their feathers are waterproof and so dense, they trap a layer of air next to the skin. They also have a thick downy layer of feathers and a layer of blubber under the skin. Penguins are superb swimmers and are more at home swimming than walking on land.

gentoo penguin

chinstrap penguin

adélie penguin

macaroni penguin

rockhopper penguin

king penguin

emperor penguin

The snow petrel and the Antarctic petrel can breed on rocky outcrops on the ice sheets several hundred kilometres inland. All petrels have thick plumage and webbed feet. Many of them nest on islands surrounding Antarctica, in burrows or cracks in the rocks.

The wandering albatross is a large bird with a wingspan of more than 3.3m (11ft). This bird spends most of its life on the wing. It breeds every other year and lays just one egg. The chicks' early life is very hard and unless there is enough good food over half of them will die. But to compensate for this the adults have a long life, up to 80 or 85 years.

Skuas live in the southern seas as well as the northern. Here, too, they are aggressive, preying on penguin colonies and stealing eggs and young birds to feed their own young.

The terns of the Antarctic breed on the Antarctic islands. Their population is boosted annually by the arrival of the terns from the Arctic, (see page 19).

The emperor is the largest penguin at just over one metre (3 ft) tall.

It is the odd one out in that it lays its egg during the winter. All the other penguins lay theirs at the start of the brief summer to be ready to go to sea for the winter. The male emperor looks after the egg, keeping it warm tucked under a fold of skin on top of his feet. For two months during the worst winter blizzards thousands of male emperor penguins huddle together to keep themselves and their eggs warm. For these two months they do not eat at all.

While the male incubates the egg, the female is away at sea catching food. She returns to the male just as the egg hatches. Her crop (a special pouch in her neck) is full of food to feed the new chick. The male can then leave and fatten himself up. The female's food lasts a few weeks, then the parents take it in turns.

The Adélie penguins nest during the summer in huge rookeries. The birds sit just out of pecking reach on nests of stone. The female lays two eggs and then returns to the sea to feed. The male incubates the eggs for two weeks and then takes it in turns with the female. The chicks stay together in nurseries looked after by an 'auntie' while they are growing. Stray chicks will be caught by a skua for food for its own chicks.

All penguins are most at risk when they are at sea. There they can become the prey of leopard seals and killer whales.

Whales

The blue whale is the largest animal to have ever lived on earth. It grows up to about 25m (81ft) long. It feeds on krill, some of the smallest creatures in the ocean.

Calves are 7.5m (24ft) long at birth and they grow very quickly. There are now about 1,000 blue whales left since many thousands were hunted for their blubber, to make oil, and for their balleen.

The humpback whales also migrate to the krill-rich waters for the summer. They feed only in cold waters.

Humpback whales are famous for their long complicated songs. They also 'breach' more frequently than other whales. 'Breaching' is when they appear to leap out of the water, often just for sheer enjoyment.

krill

The killer whale is really the largest member of the dolphin family. The baby killer whale is about 2.4m (7½ft) long when it is born and the male grows to a length of about 9.4m (30ft).

Killer whales gather in groups called pods and form a hunting group. They kill and eat seabirds, fish, seals, sharks, dolphins and will even attack a whale much bigger than themselves.